# Curing Works

The museum occupies the premises of the Tower Fish Curing Works, originally built *c.* 1850 and enlarged in 1880. The works closed in 1988 and in the following year it was first suggested that the building would be an appropriate location for a museum to tell the story of Great Yarmouth and its herring industry, the lingering aroma of the smokehouse giving it unique character. It was purchased in 1998 and £4.7 million was spent in converting the former curing works into a museum and installing the displays. After two years of work on the project it opened in July 2004.

ABOVE **The reception area occupies the coopers' workshop of the Tower Curing Works where thousands of oak barrels were made and repaired each year**
BELOW **The layout of the Tower Curing works, late 1800s**

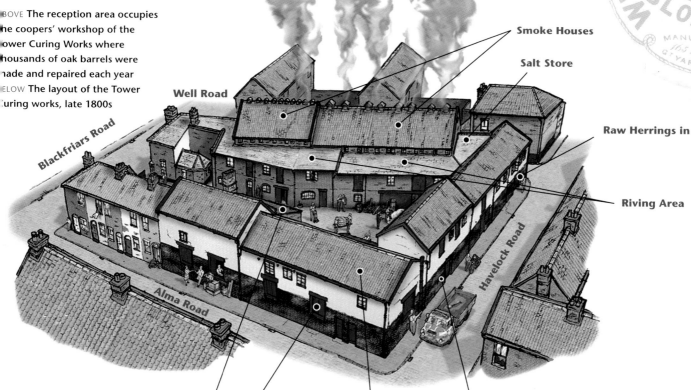

Smoke Houses

Salt Store

Raw Herrings in

Riving Area

Well Road

Blackfriars Road

Havelock Road

Alma Road

Coopers Workshop    Raw Herrings in    Storage Area    Cold Store post 1920

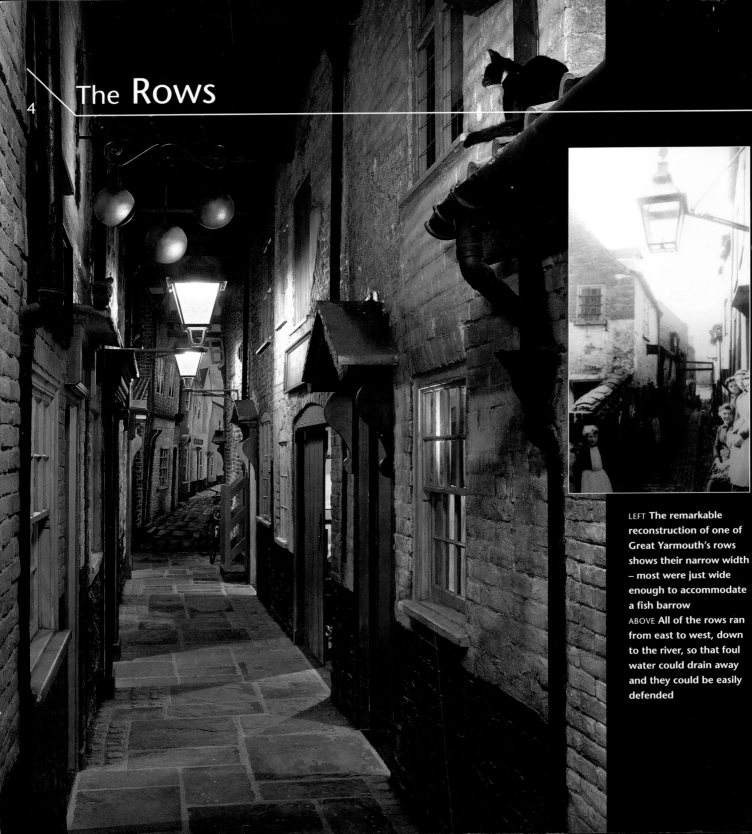

# The ROWS

LEFT **The remarkable reconstruction of one of Great Yarmouth's rows shows their narrow width – most were just wide enough to accommodate a fish barrow**

ABOVE **All of the rows ran from east to west, down to the river, so that foul water could drain away and they could be easily defended**

Great Yarmouth is famous for its 'Rows' – a series of alleyways, some of them less than a metre (3 ft) wide – which originally separated medieval tenements. Squeezed on to a narrow spit of land between sea and river and enclosed by town walls, Yarmouth in the 11th century was short of space; the close packing of buildings (domestic and trade) along narrow rows was a solution. By the end of the Middle Ages, there were about 150 rows, 145 of which remained until the outbreak of the Second World War. Enemy bombs brought an end to many of them and after the war nearly all of the surviving dwellings were demolished to make way for housing more suitable for the post-war generation.

A typical Row has been re-created here, as seen in 1913, complete with models of people who might have lived there. There is the pawnbroker Mr Curry and Harry Buckle, a retired seafarer. Alice Lamb is the widow of a drifterman and fundraiser for the Royal National Mission for Deep Sea Fisherman (RNMDSF). Mr Chambers has fallen on hard times. He is a sailmaker, but the days of sail are numbered as the drifting fleet is converted to steam power. Eliza Swan, pregnant with her second child, wonders where the next penny will come from. She lets out the spare room through the autumn to Scots girls who follow the herring southwards and pay her three shillings

RIGHT **Mr Chambers the sailmaker sits in his workshop contemplating the sad state of his trade as steam drifters take over from sailing vessels**
FAR RIGHT **Eliza Swan makes her little home ready for seasonal lodgers – a pair of Scottish herring girls**

each for their accommodation. Harry and Alice Fellows are shrimpers and have to work hard through the summer to supply visitors with Great Yarmouth's famous pink shrimps. Cats in the Rows used to feed themselves by stealing fish from the quay and were not much interested in catching rats or mice.

ABOVE **A kitten watches the goings-on in the row from the window of Mrs Lamb's sitting room, unaware of the pigeon above the pawnbroker's doorway (right)**
BOTTOM RIGHT **The strange creature in a glass case is an Old Man Fish**

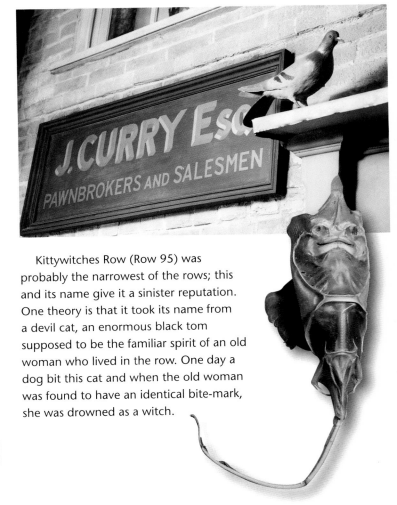

## Charles Marsh

Great Yarmouth had nearly 200 pubs and beerhouses in the 1860s, many of them in the Rows. The Half Moon, in Row 29, was famous for its concert room where Charles Marsh, violinist and acrobat, used to perform. In May 1863 he decided to attract publicity by playing his violin from the head of Britannia at the top of Nelson's Monument, 44m (144 ft) above the ground. The performance proved to be the finale to Marsh's career as on his descent he slipped from Britannia's shoulder and fell to his death.

Kittywitches Row (Row 95) was probably the narrowest of the rows; this and its name give it a sinister reputation. One theory is that it took its name from a devil cat, an enormous black tom supposed to be the familiar spirit of an old woman who lived in the row. One day a dog bit this cat and when the old woman was found to have an identical bite-mark, she was drowned as a witch.

# The Fishwharf

ABOVE **Herrings awaiting auction on the quay c. 1910. Each basket held a cran of herring (178 kg/392 lb)**
RIGHT **The scene on the fishwharf shows baskets, barrels and boxes of fish**
BELOW *View of Yarmouth Fishwharf*, 1873, by Charles J. Watson, 1854–1927

Before 1869 the Great Yarmouth fishing boats either unloaded their catches on the beach into carts drawn up alongside them on the sands, or used the jetty of the harbour. This was built in 1560 and heralded Great Yarmouth's re-emergence as a seaport. When the railway came to the town in 1844, it brought the prospect of new, more distant, markets for the fish trade. Later, c. 1880, steam tugs began to be used to allow fishing boats (all of them still sail-powered) to reach their berths more easily and to be left, whatever the state of wind or tide.

# The Fishwharf

The new fishwharf had a long length of wide quay with a covered market, offices and refreshment rooms plus sheds in which baskets and other gear were stowed. In 1882 railway lines along the quay were connected to the main lines serving the town so that the fishing industry could transport fresh fish direct to London.

At the end of September, as the last holidaymakers were leaving the boarding houses, their places were taken by workers from Scotland, most of them women, who followed the fishing fleet southwards as the shoals of herring migrated. As many as 6,000 Scottish lassies swelled the town's population in the busiest seasons and special overnight trains ran from Aberdeen to bring them to Great Yarmouth. A lot of the Scots girls worked in teams of three on the quay with two of them gutting the fish with a deft flick of their knives while the third graded them and packed them into barrels. Some could gut 60 herrings in a minute. Other girls worked at repairing the nets, and a small army of men also travelled south with the girls to make barrels and baskets and help in the curing works.

BOTTOM **Scene depicting herring being unloaded at the fishwharf in 1955 when Great Yarmouth handled some 60 million herring from 150 boats. Sadly, the start of the decline followed**
BELOW *A Slack Day at the Quay for the Scots girls*, by Stephen Batchelder, *c.* 1900

# Fishing for Herring

Once the fishing industry began at Yarmouth in Norman times, herring became an important part of people's diet and was widely enjoyed. King Edward I (1272–1307) granted a lease of land at Carlton (near Lowestoft) on condition he was provided with 24 portions of freshly caught herring. Herring was eaten by the archers fighting the Battle of Agincourt in 1415 as well as by the English sailors confronting the Spanish Armada in 1588.

By the 19th century herring was consumed more by poor people, particularly in winter when meat, much harder to preserve, cost far more than they could afford. Although we now know that herring is a wonderfully healthy foodstuff, 200 years ago those who relied on it in order to live often complained about its bones and oiliness. Even some fishermen disliked eating their catch, though others relished it and one of the 'drivers' (an engineer in the early days of steam) regularly ate ten of them for his breakfast.

An interactive display illustrates the helmsman's view during a North Sea storm

TOP **The herring were steeped in salty brine on arrival at the curing works**
ABOVE **A drifter's nameboard**
RIGHT **The crest of Bloomfields, owners of a large fishing fleet at Great Yarmouth until 1962**

# Fishing for Herring

Herring rise to the surface to feed off plankton in the latter part of the day. Millions of them swim in shoals five or six kilometres long (three or four miles) and at least three kilometres (two miles) wide and, until the 1950s, their autumnal migration took them southwards from the east coast of Scotland through the North Sea fishing grounds off Norfolk and Suffolk and on to their winter spawning grounds in the Dover Straits and off Brittany. Over the centuries, fishermen developed skills that helped them to locate the shoals, catching them with drift nets suspended from the surface of the sea. Each net was 12 metres (39 ft) deep by 32 metres (105 ft) long and 100 or more of them were joined together so that the boat might well end up nearly three kilometres (two miles) away from the end of its nets. As the fish pursued the plankton the cotton mesh of the net caught them by the gills and held them there until the crew drew up the net and took the herring off it.

This way of fishing was friendly to the environment for two reasons. Firstly, few fish other than herring were caught in the nets; secondly, drifting, as its name implied, used little fuel as the boat only had to follow its nets and avoid other shipping.

BELOW **A lively painting by Tom Swan, fl.1895–1914, of a Great Yarmouth steam drifter hauling nets off Smith's Knoll lightship**

LEFT **Model of a 'fifie', typical of the Scottish boats that used to follow the herring south before the advent of steam**

LEFT **The boat that netted the single largest catch in the season won the Prunier Trophy and could wear this pennant on its masthead**
RIGHT **A model of the steam drifter *Young John*, built at Yarmouth in 1914, with its mizzen sail set**

Unhappily, some fishing fleets began to convert to trawling in the 1950s, with more powerful diesel boats dragging vast trawl nets over the seabed to dredge up all marine life, useful or otherwise. Most of the catch was used for pig and poultry food and only a small proportion reached the fish market. Was it a coincidence that the east coast herring fishery suddenly declined as the trawlers took over?

In the days of sail many of the deckhands were labourers from Norfolk and Suffolk farms who joined the fleet after harvest was ended. They were known as joskins and easily had the strength required to man the winches to haul in the huge nets that were heavy with the volume of herring and sodden with seawater and fish-oil. After the herring had been taken off them the nets needed to be cleaned and then stowed above the catch in the hold. If this was not done properly, the hemp of the net could react with the fish-oil and combust spontaneously.

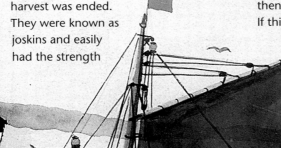

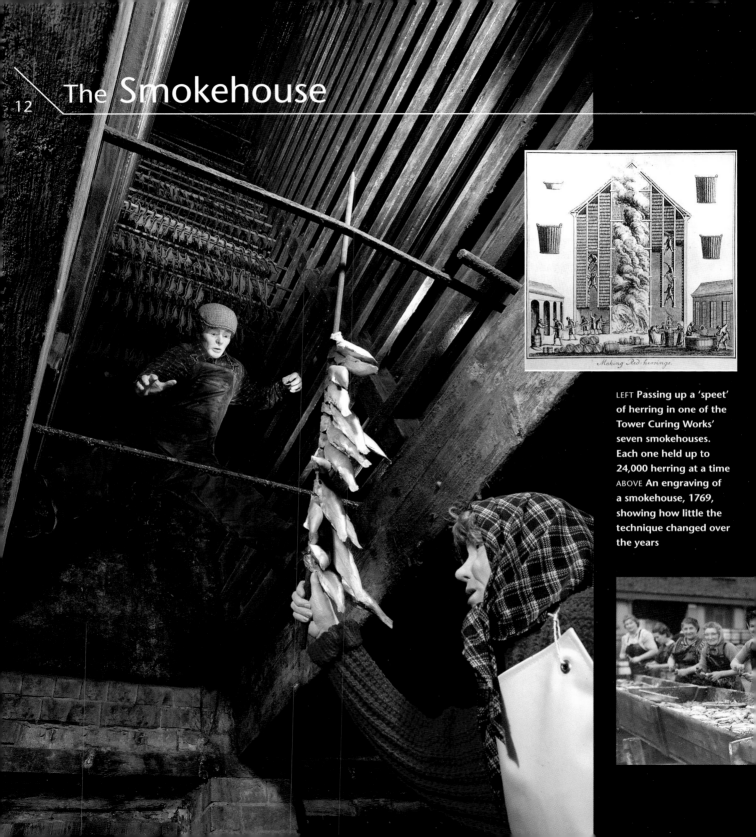

*Making Red-herrings.*

LEFT **Passing up a 'speet' of herring in one of the Tower Curing Works' seven smokehouses. Each one held up to 24,000 herring at a time** ABOVE **An engraving of a smokehouse, 1769, showing how little the technique changed over the years**

Salt was used to preserve fish at the time when Yarmouth arose from the sea. Freshly-caught fish were sprinkled with a small amount of salt, a very precious commodity in those days. A Dutchman, William Beukels, is usually credited with inventing the basis of proper fish curing in 1386. He gutted his herring immediately it was caught and packed them into barrels, covering each layer with salt. This simple method quickly made the Dutch the masters of the North Sea fishery and they held this position until Britain took it after winning naval supremacy in the North Sea in the 18th century. In the 1860s Scottish curers opened up lucrative markets in the Mediterranean for these so-called 'pickled' herrings. However, Great Yarmouth soon stole a large share of this trade as its herrings, caught at the end of their migration, were less oily. Most of the exports from the Tower Curing Works went to Italy.

If you came to Great Yarmouth on holiday you were as likely to send a box of bloaters to your loved ones as a postcard. Shops in Regent Road specialized in meeting this demand and just before the Second World War 5,000 boxes a day were handled by the Post Office. Visitors usually chose bloaters, ungutted, gently smoked fish that were less oily and salty than red herrings. The latter used to be the town's speciality and got their colour from a long smoking lasting seven days. They were a popular pub food as their saltiness made customers thirsty. There were also kippers, said to have been invented by John Woodger in 1846 at Seahouses in the Northeast, which are split open before being smoked. Woodger had premises in Great Yarmouth; at the end of the 1890s he was smoking 20 million kippers each year just for sale in London. Pickling, or salting, herring is the oldest method of preserving them and herring treated in this way were exported to places as far apart as Russia, Italy, Greece, and even the plantations of the West Indies.

# The Town that grew out of the Sea

Nomadic people searched for food around the site of Great Yarmouth more than half a million years ago. At that time Britain was still connected to mainland Europe, but geological change created the North Sea; when the glaciers melted after the Ice Age, sea levels rose. They were more or less stable by Roman times, but a vast estuary covered the ground where Great Yarmouth stands today. The Romans recognized the strategic importance of the estuary with its safe anchorages and built forts at Caister and Burgh Castle to protect it.

At the end of Roman times, the sea level had begun to fall and a sand spit was steadily growing southwards from Caister. Enterprising fishermen used this as a place to dry their nets and a handful of them built huts. Over the centuries, as the dry area steadily increased, more and more settled permanently; by the time William I arrived from Normandy, a thriving fishing and trading community had become established.

Originally, the wardens of the Cinque Ports on the south coast controlled the fishing that supported Great Yarmouth. The town's fishermen disputed these rights and the rival factions often fought each other until, in 1340, Edward III brought an end to hostilities, deciding that the fishing

LEFT **An early flint hand axe found at Horsey**
RIGHT **Stone coffin found on the site of Blackfriars Priory**
BELOW **A Roman coin with the head of Constantius I, Emperor** AD **307–12**

LEFT **The smell of the smokehouse lingers in this gallery that contains artefacts, paintings and tableaux illustrating the history of Great Yarmouth**

Scroby Sands shelters Great Yarmouth from the full force of an offshore wind and in the days of sail the channel between the sands and the shore offered the only secure anchorage where east-coast shipping might ride out a severe north-easterly storm. Occasionally, even this refuge was unsafe, and in the 18th century Daniel Defoe wrote of 140 vessels being wrecked out of 200 sheltering there from a gale.

Captain Manby was in charge of the barracks at Great Yarmouth. He witnessed a shipwreck in 1807 where 67 people drowned. He invented a very succesful method of shooting a line to a stricken vessel. The 'Breeches Buoy' (above right) was another method of saving lives. Two lines were fired from the shore to the ship, with the other end anchored to the shore on a tower. The buoy was sent to and fro, using a pulley system.

## The 'Sudan' Hen

This hen was rescued from the *Sudan*, a ship that came to grief on Scroby Sands in 1895. The Gorleston lifeboat also rescued all of the crew of the *Sudan* and in gratitude the skipper presented the hen to its coxswain. Her good fortune was short-lived: the coxswain had her killed and stuffed as a memento.

grounds belonged to Great Yarmouth. This good fortune was clouded by the steady growth of a sandbank across the entrance to the harbour. Efforts were made to keep it clear by dredging, but storms soon piled the sand back and when the Black Death killed 7,000 out of its population of 10,000, Great Yarmouth had neither the means nor the manpower to keep the channel clear. The following two centuries saw six unsuccessful attempts at dredging a new channel, but in the end Great Yarmouth's saviour was a Dutchman, Johas Johnson, who between 1559 and 1567 succeeded in creating the outlet to the sea that is still in use today.

ABOVE **A jug bearing the likeness of Cardinal Bellarmine (1542–1621), made in Italy c. 1700. One of many found at Great Yarmouth**

ABOVE A "What the Butler Saw' machine (this one presenting a shoot-out from a cowboy film)
LEFT A young visitor listens to the story of how Great Yarmouth became one of Britain's most popular holiday destinations
BELOW An array of buckets, spades and moulds for creating shapes in the sand

changed almost overnight. Day trippers who enjoyed promenading and sitting on the beach replaced the well-heeled visitors who had formerly come for the beneficial effects of bracing air and healthy sea bathing. As the railway network developed, Great Yarmouth became the venue for works outings from the factories of the Midlands.

The influx of thousands of trippers meant that Great Yarmouth had to provide amusements and entertainments and many of the features that we know today came into being – the piers, scenic railway and boating lake are all examples. The cinemas and theatres were for people staying longer than just a day, and more of them did so as holidays became more usual after the First World War. Most people lodged in boarding houses situated close to the seafront in the rooms occupied by fisher girls in the autumn. The years just before and after the Second World War were the heyday of Great Yarmouth as a resort. With its four miles of golden sands, its long promenade and sheltered gardens, and the spectacular entertainments on offer, it became the east-coast rival of Blackpool.

Sea bathing began to become popular with the upper classes in the mid 18th century and in 1759 a bath house was built on the beach at Great Yarmouth that provided two baths just large enough for men and women to immerse themselves in seawater. A little later, horse-drawn bathing huts were trundled into the waves and their occupants (either men or women, never both) could swim or splash about in the waves out of sight of bystanders on the beach. This was just as well: until the 1850s, men bathed naked.

When the railway came to Great Yarmouth in 1844 the clientele of the resort

TOP, LEFT AND RIGHT **Old playbills, china souvenirs, postcards and holidaymakers arriving by train are reminders of the golden age of the seaside resort**

# Great Yarmouth a **Trading** Town

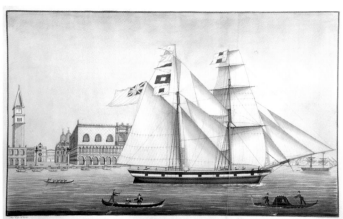

BRIGANTINE ISIS, JOSEPH PRESS, COMMANDER, LEAVING THE PORT OF VENICE 1851

Before the railways, it was much quicker to travel long distances by sea rather than overland, and it was easily the only efficient way of transporting goods. Great Yarmouth's position gave it a great advantage in trading to the Low Countries but its shipowners steadily expanded their influence; by the 19th century, their vessels were reaching every continent. The port was also strategically important for the navy's control of the North Sea and Nelson, being Norfolk born and bred,

had a particular fondness for it. He landed at Great Yarmouth after his triumphs at the Battle of the Nile in 1800 and the Battle of Copenhagen in 1801.

Wherries played an important part in taking Great Yarmouth cargoes to and from remote parts of Norfolk and Suffolk. Their shallow draught and single large sail made them ideal for the twisting waterways linking the Broads. If the wind failed their crew had to push them along with a quant-pole until they turned the bend of a reach and picked up a whisper of wind. They carried a variety of goods to and from seagoing ships lying at the Great Yarmouth quays, and canals were dug to allow them to reach places like Bungay and North Walsham.

TOP LEFT **Shipowners sometimes paid artists to show their vessels in exotic locations. The brig** Isis **leaving Venice, 1851**
ABOVE **A Lacon's Brewery sign. Their brewery on Church Plain sent 2–3,000 barrels of beer to London each week in the 1850s**
BELOW *The Mackerel Market on the Beach,* **by Robert Ladbrooke, 1810**

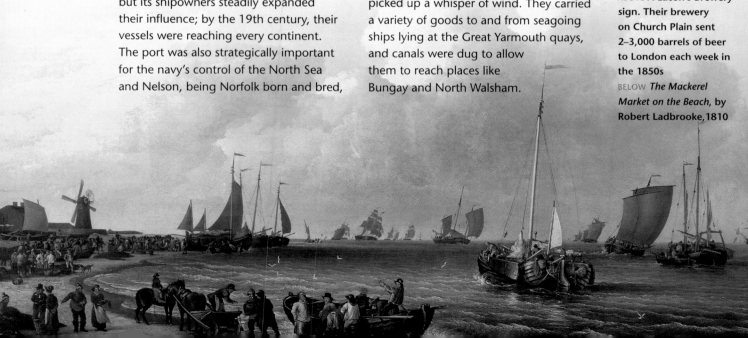

# Maritime Trades

Support workers were vital to the fishing industry. Shipwrights built the boats that the fishermen sailed in and in the 19th century 600 of them were employed at Great Yarmouth making wooden sailing ships not just for local fishermen but for fleets throughout Britain. Baskets were vital in unloading and measuring the catch – fishermen preferred new ones as they held less fish before they stretched. The standard basket (Quarter Cran) was introduced by

the Scots in 1908 as the official measurement and held a quarter of a cran of herring (44 kg/97 lb). Great Yarmouth had distinctively-shaped baskets called swills that held two-thirds of a cran. Wooden boxes were also important and the Great Yarmouth firm of Jewson supplied some of the wood.

Many hundreds of women worked at repairing nets, in net houses on the South Denes. They were called beatsters and their job was to mend the tears in hundreds of miles of nets, using hand-sized beating needles to knot new meshes. Nets also had to be degreased in salt water before being boiled in a creosote mixture called 'cutch' to preserve them. (Cutch is the bark of the East Indian betal-nut palm.)

ABOVE LEFT **Making herring baskets or swills from locally-grown osiers**

ABOVE **Scene showing some maritime trades including repairing nets and basket making**

LEFT **Scrimshaws were crafted by seafarers in their free time at sea. Carved on the tooth of a sperm whale, this one shows whaling scenes**

## Box making

The Tower Curing Works was large enough to have its own box-making machine (left) but smaller merchants had them made by specialist box-makers who were sometimes called upon to supply much larger containers. In wartime they made boxes for ammunition, guns and even aircraft parts. Jewson's wood-yard supplied softwood for boxes as well as oak for barrels and shruff (oak shavings and sawdust) for the smokehouses. Jewson's have become a leading supplier of goods to the building trade.

## Zeppelin

The Zeppelin was an ideal weapon for spreading panic in a civilian population. They came by night, silently descending from 6,000m (20,000 ft) to drop bombs on

towns and cities. Until the introduction of incendiary ammunition in 1916 they ruled the skies where their limited range allowed them to operate. Flight-Lieutenant Egbert Cadbury became a war hero when he shot down the L70, the most famous Zeppelin of all, on 5 August 1918. Shortly afterwards the final Zeppelin raid of the war was foiled by Great Yarmouth-based aircraft.

The season before the outbreak of the First World War saw the Great Yarmouth fishing industry at its peak. The herrings swam in enormous shoals and were caught by the largest fishing fleet ever seen in these waters, at least 1,100 boats taking part. In total, 1,359,213 crans of herring were landed at Great Yarmouth in the autumn of 1913 – at least 160 million fish.

The holiday season was at its height when war broke out in August 1914. With a submarine base and a naval air station, Great Yarmouth was an obvious target and history was made on 19 January 1915 when a Zeppelin airship dropped nine bombs and demolished a house in St Peter's Plain. Two people died, the first to be killed in Britain by an attack from the sky. Although there were further air-raids and bombardments from the sea in which four people died, the town suffered most from the disruption brought to its fishing and holiday industries.

The years following the war saw more people taking holidays at the seaside. Fishing remained important though the catches were rarely as good as those taken before the war. There was more time to prepare for the Second World War, yet Great Yarmouth suffered severely: 217 people died in air raids and more than 1,600 houses were damaged beyond repair. Great Yarmouth was a favourite target for enemy bombers as it was comparatively close to Germany and had an important naval base. Fast motor gun boats sailed from the harbour to protect

LEFT **An Edwardian recruiting poster**
BELOW **A collection of Second World War magazines**
FAR RIGHT **A house in Salisbury Road badly damaged by the raid on 29 July, 1942**

North Sea convoys, while minelayers and minesweepers (many of them converted fishing boats) also operated from the port. Fortunately, most children and their mothers living in Great Yarmouth were evacuated at the beginning of hostilities when it was thought that the Norfolk coast would be a likely landing-place for an invasion fleet.

During the Second World War, herring fishing was based on the west coast of Britain, but afterwards it soon resumed at Great Yarmouth, although catching mines in the nets proved to be hazardous at first. Coronation year,1953, saw disastrous flooding along the east coast but proved to be a good year for the boats. Catches dwindled in the following years so that by the 1960s hardly any Scottish boats fished from Great Yarmouth, whose own fleet was a shadow of what it had been previously. The discovery of offshore oil and gas fields compensated for this decline and Great Yarmouth suddenly became a boom town with great numbers of oil workers from all over the world seeking accommodation.

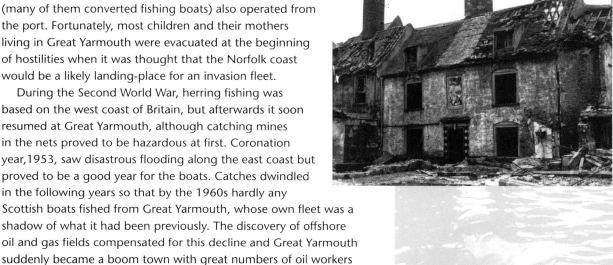

LEFT **The Morrison shelter became a common feature of the living room during the Second World War. It was intended to defend against falling masonry rather than a direct hit by a bomb**
BACKGROUND PICTURE **The tidal surge on the night of 31 January 1953 swept away the Breydon sea wall and flooded 3,500 homes in Southtown. Ten people died in Great Yarmouth and many more around the east coast from Hunstanton to Canvey Island**

# The Future: from Herrings to Heritage

The herring fishing trade (at its height just before the First World War in 1913) gradually started to decline. The next slow decline happened to the holiday trade (in its heyday before and after the Second World War), due to the rapidly growing package holiday business.

In the last three decades of the 20th century, Great Yarmouth enjoyed economic growth as the great oil companies vied with each other in prospecting and exploiting the offshore gas fields. Many people are surprised that the town retains so much of the industry today, but worthwhile business remains for companies servicing the pipelines and platforms.

Now, alternative energy from renewable sources has arrived at Great Yarmouth in the form of a huge wind farm off Scroby Sands.

The future of the town looks bright, if the proposal for the new outer harbour is adopted (see opposite). Hopefully, 'EastPort' will be operational in 2008, with a roll-on roll-off ferry operating

The Old Merchant's House, Row 111 South Quay. Beautiful 17th-century house with fine plasterwork and oak paneling, saved from demolition in 1936 by local enthusiasts

The Tolhouse was originally the home of a prosperous 12th-century merchant. Later it became the town courthouse and gaol. Today it has displays and artefacts illustrating the history of Great Yarmouth with particular emphasis on crime and punishment

The Elizabethan House, 4 South Quay. A museum of domestic life set in a beautiful quayside house dating from 1596. Its Victorian kitchen is a memorable feature